HELP!
I'M IN A CONFLICT

Ernie Baker

Consulting Editor: Dr. Paul Tautges

© 2014 Ernie Baker

ISBN
Paper: 978-1-63342-078-6
ePub: 978-1-63342-079-3
Kindle: 978-1-63342-080-9

Shepherd Press
P.O. Box 24
Wapwallopen, PA 18660

www.shepherdpress.com

All Scripture quotations, unless stated otherwise, are from the New American Standard Bible (1995)

First printed by Day One Publications

Designed by **documen**

CONTENTS

INTRODUCTION

Sleepless nights, loss of appetite, broken relationships, and emotions going crazy with anger, bitterness, and anxiety all describe times of conflict. Add to this nasty e-mails, accusations flying, and people getting "defriended" on social networking sites. These reactions cause many to ask questions like, "How can Christians treat each other this way?" "How did my marriage get to this point?" "Why does God allow such conflict in His church?" "If this is what the church is like I don't want to have anything to do with it!"

Right from the very beginning the history of the planet has included conflict. Unfortunately, churches and Christians are not immune. In fact, the statistics on the Evangelical Church in the United States are appalling. One study has shown that of all evangelical churches polled, 34% percent forced their previous pastor to resign, and 23% of all current pastors in the U.S. have been fired or forced to resign. One of the most troubling statistics of all is that the average pastoral career lasts only fourteen years. [1] Though these statistics are incredibly sad they do not include all of the marriages feeling tension, families fighting over inheritance, or nations at war.

How are we supposed to respond to others when we are in conflict? What kind of guidance can the Bible give us? Does gospel-grounded truth address tension in our relationships? What practical steps should we take if we're experiencing relationship difficulty? These are some of the questions this mini-book will answer.

1

No Stranger to Conflict

Conflict is much more than an academic subject for me. As a pastor, I am not a stranger to conflict. In fact, the tensest moments in my life have been spent in congregational or church board meetings!

Many years ago, a group of people within my church began to express their concerns about my leadership. They wrote letters of complaint and "voted with their pocketbooks" as they withheld their giving. Many accusations were made, among which was that I was not a loving pastor. I was also told by the music committee that they should have more money in the budget. But the missions committee believed *they* were the most important because "really spiritual" churches spend more on missions. Those leading the youth ministry didn't agree; they thought they should get more because they were preparing the next generation for the Lord.

Seeking Help from a Mediator

As things intensified, the congregation became deeply divided and it became painfully obvious that we needed the help of an outside mediator. So we called a ministry that supposedly specialized in these types of situations.[2] From the beginning of this organization's involvement I realized biblical principles were being violated. For example, the "mediator" never asked me my side of the story even though Proverbs 18:17 makes it clear there is "always two sides to every story."

> *"The first to plead his case seems just,*
> *until another comes and examines him."*

The mediator also told me that his methodology was to just let people "ventilate." In other words, they just needed to get it out so that they would feel better. I can tell you there was a lot of sinful "ventilating" that violated what Scripture says about controlling the tongue. He wanted me to not attend a congregational meeting so that people could freely stand and share concerns about me, which was a direct violation of Matthew 18:15, "And if your brother sins, go and reprove him in private; if he listens to you, you have won your brother."

This experience was a shock to me as a pastor. I had grown up in a pastor's home and knew, at least in theory, the potential of church conflict since I had seen my father go through much of it. I had led myself to believe, however, that if I did all my duties as a pastor and preached solid biblical messages that everyone would love me. I found out the painful way that this is not true.

The reality set in when I started to receive anonymous letters. After a while I began to check first to see if the letter was signed. If it was not I would throw it away because I believed anonymity violated the biblical principle to go to your brother personally if you have a concern.

I know from this experience, and others like it, that it is easy for cynicism and thoughts of failure to rise. Maybe you've had these or other similar things go through your mind. "I'm a failure as a wife." Or, "They fired me, I must be a failure." Cynicism can eat away at your soul and you can grow hard, not wanting to be hurt again. It is easy then to put up barriers of self-protection and not let others get close. Pastors then drop out of ministry and others drop out of their marriages.

If these or similar experiences and emotions have been yours then I am writing to you. It is my hope that you will be encouraged as you see what the Lord may be doing and as you realize how relevant Scripture is for dealing with tensions in relationships. In fact, the topic of broken relationships comes up near the beginning of the Scriptures and reveals to us how desperately we need the Lord to intervene and provide answers. Let's start at the beginning and see where tension in relationships originated.

The Origin of Conflict

To understand how drastic the situation has become let's contrast it with what life may have been like in the pre-conflict, sin-free world. Genesis 1:26-28 tell us that as humans we were created with the high privilege of portraying the image of God. According to these verses this image is uniquely reflected in a man and woman coming together as husband and wife. Just as God the Father, Son, and Holy Spirit are in harmony with one another the first husband and wife were to reflect this by being in harmony with one another. There was no tension, only harmony. There was no turmoil, only peace. Sound amazing? Can you even imagine any relationship being like that?

This sense of what it may been like before the events of Genesis 3 is reinforced further by chapter two telling us that this new husband and wife were "one flesh" and "naked and... not ashamed" (2:24-25). In other words, there was nothing between them, not even clothes. Wow! Things were about to change radically.

Broken relationships are right at the heart of what happened next, described in Genesis 3. Because of their mistrust of God, Adam and Eve had a new, and I'm sure very uncomfortable, experience of tension in their relationship. But an infinitely more devastating result of their lack of following the Lord was the break in their relationship with Him!

First, notice some of the heart-wrenching impact on relationships. After sin entered Adam and Eve's world...

1. They covered themselves and hid from God (3:7). There were now barriers in relationships.

2. They blamed others for their problems (3:12).

3. Tension entered into the husband's and wife's particular roles (3:16-17).

4. And, to top it off, just a few verses later, a brother murdered his brother (4:8).

Painful as these things are, however, the most

heartbreaking aspect is the loss of relationship with their Creator. They distrusted Him, misquoted Him, hid from Him, lied to Him, and consequently were removed from the garden of Eden (3:24). There were now not only barriers between the man and his wife but the man and his Creator. It is imperative for us to realize that the tensions we experience daily are rooted here, in the first human rebellion.

As I've thought about this passage of Scripture through the years I have been amazed at the Lord's mercy toward Adam and Eve. In the immediate aftermath of their rebellion He promised them that someone would come and defeat the serpent (3:15). Scripture then unfolds this amazing story of the coming Savior and His finished work on the cross and all its implications, both for life now and an eternity of perfect relationships with God and others.

Scripture, Not Naïve about Conflict

But does the story of Christ's death, burial and resurrection really apply to my conflict? Apparently the Apostle Paul thought so since he addressed tension in relationships quite often in his writings, as we see from the following examples. He always writes against the backdrop of what our Lord did through his death and resurrection, and who we are relation to him. Often his commands relate to how the gospel (good news) impacts relationships. Quite regularly, relationship tension is at least implied in the context.

1 Corinthians

The Corinthian church had a notorious reputation for conflict (and a lot of other problems as well)! Because of this, the book of 1 Corinthians was written and the Corinthian Christians reputation will continue until the end of time. In seminary, I was encouraged to make 1 Corinthians the first book I preached through when going to a new church since it addresses so many contemporary issues in the local church. That way, no one could accuse me of knowing, and preaching about, what was actually going on!

In the first chapter, Paul gently confronts the Corinthians:

> For I have been informed concerning you,
> my brethren, by Chloe's people that there
> are quarrels among you" (verse 11).

Later, in 6:1, he addresses the specific question

of lawsuits:

> *Does any one of you, when he has a case*
> *against his neighbor , dare to go to law*
> *before the unrighteous and not before*
> *saints?*

Brothers and sisters in Christ were taking one another to court! In other words, Paul was thinking, "How dare the just go to the unjust for justice!"

PHILIPPIANS

In Philippians, Paul writes,

> *I urge Euodia and I urge Syntyche to live*
> *in harmony in the Lord" (4:2).*

These two women needed help getting along and I assume their sour relationship was impacting the church. This may be why he wrote earlier in this letter,

> *Only conduct yourselves in a manner*
> *worthy of the gospel of Christ, so that*
> *whether I come and see you or remain*
> *absent, I will hear of you that you are*

> standing firm in one spirit, with one
> mind striving together for the faith of the
> gospel" (1:27).

We often focus on the wonderful theology concerning our Lord's sacrificial death (2:6-11) but forget that the context is yet another admonition to unity (2:1-5). In fact, I have come to the conclusion that verse 4 is one of the most important conflict resolution verses in the Bible. Based upon the example of our Lord, the apostle writes,

> Do not merely look out for your own
> personal interests, but also to the
> interests of others.

A few verses later he admonishes the believers,

> Do all things without grumbling
> or disputing; so that you will prove
> yourselves to be blameless and innocent,
> children of God above reproach in
> the midst of a crooked and perverse
> generation, among whom you appear as
> lights in the world, (2:14-15).

He wouldn't have had to remind them not to

grumble if it wasn't already happening. What motivates him is the same thing that seems to almost always motivate him—the reputation of Jesus Christ.

It is easy to see that Scripture is not naïve about conflict and gives wise direction on how to handle the inevitable tension accompanying relationships. The Bible makes clear (and it's a good reality check to understand) there never was a pristine time in the church where believers did not have to work through difficult issues.

Out of all the passages where Paul addresses relationships Ephesians 4:1-3 deserves special attention. Let's look at that next.

2

Reconciliation Needed

Ephesians 4:1-3 needs to be unpacked in more detail since its principles are so memorable and applicable to conflict. Those who desire to deal with brokenness in relationships will find that verse 3 will regularly echo in their ears:

> [Be] diligent to keep the unity of the
> Spirit in the bond of peace.

Part of the context in the book of Ephesians is Paul's address to the Jews and Gentiles who were now part of a new thing called "the church." He writes of

> the mystery of Christ, ... that the Gentiles
> are fellow heirs and fellow members of
> the body, and fellow partakers of the
> promise in Christ Jesus through the
> Gospel" (3:6).

Imagine how difficult this must have been for

his Jewish readers! Jewish people, with their strong ethnic identity, were now being asked to mix with "unclean" Gentiles in the name of Christ. Those first years of integration must have been hard for the church. Wait—they still are. Martin Luther King Jr. was right when he said that the most segregated time in America is Sunday morning!

Think about your own local church. The members probably come from different denominational backgrounds and you fellowship with people of various age groups who are at varying places of maturity physically, emotionally, and spiritually. There are diverse perspectives on what church is supposed to be and about the role of church leadership. Last, but definitely not least, there are different cultural and ethnic backgrounds all mixed together. Sounds like a recipe for "conflict stew" doesn't it?

Or, think about your marriage. You married a person with a different personality than yours. He or she came from a different family than yours. He or she probably has different interests than you. You may be saying, "You've got that right!" We are in much the same situation that Paul addresses with the church at Ephesus.

Motivation for Dealing with Relationships Differently

Paul starts off our passage by calling us to

> ...*walk in a manner worthy of the calling to which you have been called"* (4:1).

He is referring back to chapters 1 through 3, where he has clearly explained this "calling"— that is, who God says we are in relationship to him and to our Savior. What is Paul's point? It is quite logical: if you say you are in relationship with the God of the universe and Christ is the head of your life (as he is of his church, see 1:20-23), then live like it. You see, we are called to respond to relationship difficulties in a way that is remarkably different than the world's way, and this is possible because of our new relationship with Christ.[3]

Our Position in Christ

Getting a sense of how Paul divides his writing will bring greater impact to the verses we are looking at and that will help us make proper application for conflict resolution. In many of his books, the apostle starts with doctrine, in particular the work of Jesus Christ on behalf of sinners, and then addresses daily life and how these truths apply. Another way to think about this is "our position in Christ," followed by "practicing our new position."

So, let's look at Ephesians 1 and see what he says is true of us in Christ and what God has done for us through the work of our Savior.

» He has blessed us in Christ with every spiritual blessing in the heavenly places (verse 3).

» He chose us in Christ before the foundation of the world (verse 4).

» He predestined us to adoption (verse 5).

» In the Beloved (His son) we have glorious grace (verse 6).

» In Christ we have redemption...the forgiveness of our trespasses (verse 7)

» He has exhibited rich, lavish grace (verses 7-8).

Even though this list is not complete it is enough to set our hearts in awe of the grace of God. It is a partial list of our calling in the gospel, but it is plenty to give us an idea of how to walk worthy during times of conflict. Commentator F.F. Bruce puts it well when he writes, "Those who have been chosen by God to sit with Christ in the heavenly places must remember that the honor of Christ is involved in their daily lives."[4]

If I were to ask what words come to your mind when you hear the word "gospel," hopefully many of the things listed above would be named. Forgiveness, grace, love, mercy, and reconciliation are all at the heart of Christ's redemptive work and also should be at the center of our thinking so that we deal with one another properly. Ken Sande says, "Christians are the most forgiven people in the world. Therefore, we should be the most forgiving people in the world."[5]

Equally, if Christians have been shown the most grace (Paul says God has "lavished" his grace on us), we should be the most gracious people in the world. We have been shown the greatest amount of mercy, so we should be the most merciful. God has worked hard to redeem broken relationships, so we should follow his example and work hard to redeem broken relationships. In Christ, the Father accepts us into his family. So we, too, ought to be known as welcoming people.

Reconciliation Is at the Heart of the Gospel

One term, though, deserves special emphasis—
reconciliation. The doctrine of reconciliation
is the truth that God has taken the initiative,
in Christ, to restore fallen humanity back into
relationship with himself, our Creator. Notice two
important truths and how they relate to tension in
our relationships:

GOD TOOK THE INITIATIVE TO RECONCILE SINNERS TO HIMSELF.

If it were up to us it would not happen, because
sinners do not naturally move toward God (see
Romans 3:11). But God was so concerned about
his broken relationship with his creation that he
took the initiative. He moved toward us. It is very
easy when there are tensions in relationships just
to allow the tension to exist and just try to live
with it. Therefore, if you feel a tendency to move
away from someone, it is easy to see that you do
not have a gospel-centered approach to resolving
tension in your relationships.

RECONCILIATION CAME AT GREAT PERSONAL SACRIFICE.

God the Father, gave his best. He gave us his Son.
Both absorbed great personal loss to restore our
relationship and rescue us from our sin. This same

principle will probably hold true for you as well. We show the value of a relationship by what we are willing to sacrifice for it!

Since God in Christ moved toward you, a sinner, a crucial question for you is: Will you move toward Him? He invites you to believe the message about his Son being the Savior of the world by admitting that you have been a rebel against his purposes. Before we go on thinking about how Ephesians applies to conflict resolution, why don't you stop and acknowledge to God your need of Jesus Christ as your Savior. Humble yourself before him by admitting your sin and thanking Him that He died to pay the penalty for this sin and then rose again so that you can have a new life (see Romans 10: 9-13; Romans 6 and 1 Corinthians 15:1-3 to see what God says we need to believe and what happens when we humbly admit our need of salvation). When Jesus Christ becomes the Lord of your life, you have a whole new potential for change in the way you look at relationships. Let's think about that next.

3

Attitude *is* Everything

Do you wonder why someone is so impatient with you? Or maybe you ask yourself, "Why is he/she so harsh?" Better yet, though, why are *you* impatient with certain people? Why do *you* speak harshly? We're about to answer these questions, but first we need to understand why Paul starts Ephesians 4 with a list of character traits (4:2).

Of all the things he could have started the "good works" section of the book with (chapters 4–6; see 2:10), Paul chose to begin by calling us to the reality that our relationship with Christ should impact our relationships with one another. When I used to think of "good works," the things that would come to mind were teaching Sunday School, leading in the youth ministry, going on door-to-door visitation, and giving money to the poor. But these ministry activities do not top Paul's good-works list. He starts with character traits that are to be impacted by the gospel as we relate to others. He tells us to be gentle, humble, patient, and to show forbearance toward others. This will lead us to ask important questions like the ones above: "Why am I not gentle in my relationships, in general, or in conflict, in particular?" "Why do I tend to just write people off instead of enduring their weaknesses?"

It's tempting to answer by saying, "It's just my personality. I have always been somewhat harsh." If we're content to give that answer, we're basically saying, "You'll just have to accept me the way I am. I'm just not a gentle person." Or, "I'm just not very patient." Praise God, we do have different personalities, but to accept the world's idea that our personality is unchangeable is to deny the doctrine of "progressive sanctification"—the doctrine that explains how we grow and change toward becoming like Christ, which is God's goal for us (Romans 8:29).[6] It may be true that you have natural tendencies that are the opposite of the character traits that Scripture demands, but that does not mean you cannot change. Change is possible through the power of the gospel and the Holy Spirit whom Jesus sent to indwell believers.

Changing the Way We Think about God, Ourselves, and Others

Change begins on the inside, at the level of our desires, motivations, and attitudes. It then works its way outward to our actions. The Lord is always interested, primarily, in changing our inner person, rather than our outward behavior. This is not to say that God is not interested in our behavior, he certainly is! However, since he created us he also understands how we operate, so to speak. As Jesus made clear in Mark 7:21-23,

> For from within, out of the heart of men, proceed the evil thoughts, fornications, thefts, murders, adulteries, deeds of coveting and wickedness, as well as deceit, sensuality, envy, slander, pride and foolishness. All these evil things proceed from within and defile the man.

As part of our study on the character traits listed by Paul in Ephesians 4, we will include Paul's list from Colossians 3, which is a parallel chapter. He includes many of the same character traits there, but adds a few more. So between the two chapters we'll get a good idea of the characteristic traits that are necessary for healthy relationships, which are the same ones we ought to be developing as we submit to the Lordship of Christ over our lives.

Beside each word as it is translated in the *New American Standard Bible*, I'll give a definition from a standard Greek dictionary.[7]

1. **Humility** refers to lowliness of mind, being humble-minded. Many think that Paul may have coined this term since humility was a distinctly Christian character trait. It was very unlike what was valued in the Greek culture of his day. This lowliness of mind means thinking of yourself in proper relationship to others, as a servant, and of yourself in proper relationship to God, as subject to Him. This mindset leads to thinking more of others than of oneself.

2. **Gentleness** comes from a word that is sometimes translated meekness. But the concept that I like the most is "strength under control." Our Lord described himself as "meek" but he certainly was not weak (Matthew 11:29, KJV). His "strength under control" becomes evident when we consider what He endured while suffering for our sin. He could have called angels to His support,

but He refrained (Matthew 26:53). This was as demonstration of meekness.

3. **Patience** is the ability to stay "far away from anger."

4. **Showing tolerance in love** means to endure, to "put up with," which is the product of biblical love. It could be translated "forbearance". Since "tolerance" is often misused in our society, we need to clarify that we can even lovingly put up with a person with whom we disagree.

5. **Putting on a heart of compassion**, which means to have pity or feel sympathy. It is a feeling of pain in our inner person for others and is used of our Lord in Matthew 9:36, "Seeing the people, He felt compassion for them, because they were distressed and dispirited like sheep without a shepherd."

6. **Kindness** is being generous to others for their good.

7. **Commitment** is not specifically found in either list, but the idea permeates the verses through the use of the word "tolerance" and also the phrase "being diligent to preserve the unity of the Spirit in the bond of peace." Our forbearance with

one another is based upon our Lord's continued patience with us who, even as believers, learn to work through our conflicts instead of running from them. It is encouraging and worth noting that throughout Scripture these same characteristics describe various members of the Trinity (Romans 2:4; Matthew 11:29). As we grow in these areas--because of the difference the gospel makes in our lives—we are literally becoming more "godly" or like Christ.

Taking a Look at the Opposites

It is also important for our purposes to think of the opposites of these character traits and how each actually compounds tension in our relationships. With each of these areas, I'll suggest some questions for you to ask yourself about your relationships.

1. **Pride** is the opposite of humility. It means being "high-minded." We are all guilty of thinking of ourselves more highly than we should. What does pride do when there is tension in a relationship? What comes to your mind? I think of a person who stubbornly refuses to admit his or her wrong. I think of

the person who digs his heels in and won't change his opinion. I think of the person who has to get in the last word, or who isn't really concentrating on what the other person is saying, but is just waiting for him to finish so that he can say what he believes is more important. This type of attitude escalates conflict. Our humble Savior helps us learn how to die to self and think of others as more important than ourselves (Philippians 2:3).

2. **Harshness** is the opposite of gentleness. When you talk harshly to others what typically happens? Either the person withdraws because you aren't a safe person to talk to, or they might have the opposite reaction and become louder since they want to be sure you understand that they will not let you push them around. A particular concern I have here is for men. It seems that many men are harsh with their wives or children. God gave men a deeper, more booming voice and it's easier to use it in the wrong way. Being "Mr. Tough Guy" isn't the way the Lord desires for men to treat their wives or children. One reason Christ died on the cross is to free us from living for ourselves (2 Corinthians 5:15).

This certainly includes learning to be gentle, to model strength under control.

3.   **Impatience** is a problem for many. When a person is impatient he or she will not be a good listener. When a person is impatient, he or she won't have time to really hear the other person out. This would be a good place to start thinking at an even deeper level. Why are you impatient? Why do you speak harshly? Why do you think your opinion is so important? For the Lord to really change us from the inside out we can't believe the lie of the world that it's just our genetics, or our personality. If these are lies we must turn away from, what is the truth needed to replace them in our mind? We'll answer that question below.

4.   **Intolerance** is a lack of grace toward others. Do you get your feelings hurt by others too easily? Do your toes get stepped on easily? I heard this described years ago as having "big toes!" Do you have thin skin and get hurt easily, not just by comments, but maybe it's just a look from someone? The older we grow in Christ, the more gracious we ought to become? Our toes ought to shrink. It ought to be harder to offend a mature Christian. A

bit later we'll talk about how you can become more tolerant of others as you put into practice biblical principles for dealing with relationship tension.

5. **Hard heartedness** is an unfeeling attitude toward others. When was the last time you felt deeply for the hurt of someone? A more important question, from my perspective would be, "Why don't you feel the hurts of others?" We could describe this type of person as hard-hearted instead of soft-hearted. Or maybe a better word would be aloof. Romans 12:15 tells us to "weep with those who weep." What keeps you from weeping? I'll warn you again that we can't use the excuse that it's just our personality. If these principles are true then we must believe that our Lord wants to teach us to have a more tender heart.

6. **Unkindness is obviously the opposite of kindness.** There is overlap here with speaking harshly to others, but often unkindness manifests itself in unkind actions. There are always temptations to write a nasty e-mail or to speak unkindly about the person with whom you are in conflict. You may object and say to yourself that "It's not okay for him to

speak to me that way. I have a right to defend myself." In a brief moment, we'll consider why we often feel we need to defend ourselves in conflict, but for now let's talk briefly about the idea of "rights."

Philippians 2:3-4 tell us....

"...with humility of mind regard one another as more important than yourselves; do not merely look out for your own personal interests, but also for the interests of others."

If you really regard the person you are feeling tension with as more important than yourself, and be concerned about the other person's interests, what happens to your "rights?" Often we have to die to our "rights" to practice what Scripture commands and our Lord modeled as a servant. If we are truly going to follow the Lord faithfully it will involve being a servant just as He modeled when He washed his disciples feet (John 13:1-14). What are some of the "rights" you believe you deserve? Ask, "What is the tension in this relationship about and what do I think I deserve that is associated with that tension?" Let

me give you two examples, one for men and one
for women.

Men, maybe you come home from a long day
at work and the house is a mess and the kids
are being loud. You may start to ask yourself,
"What did she do all day? Why do the kids
have to be so loud? Why can't I just have some
peace and quiet?" What your heart may really
be saying is, "I deserve some peace and quiet
after a long day at work!" In other words,
peace and quiet has become a "right" that you
think you deserve.

Ladies, how about when your husband comes
home and you've been with the kids all day
and he seems to mentally check out. Maybe
you're tempted to think, "He doesn't really
love me. If he did he would watch the kids or
he would sit down and talk to me. I've been
talking with children all day and would like
him to pay attention to me." Do you see how
you might believe you have a right to adult
conversation or a right to some down time for
yourself, which he is keeping from you by not
watching the children?

For conflict to be resolved we must learn how to

esteem others as more important than ourselves, following the example of the Lord. This type of attitude often defuses the tension in a relationship.

7. **Lack of commitment** is demonstrated by the willingness to allow relationships to wither. This could come from the frustration of just not knowing what to do to work through issues, or maybe the attitude is, "Relationships can be so frustrating. Why can't this be easier!?" Or maybe the thought goes through your mind, "If he wants to be that way I'll just have to live with it; I'm too busy to deal with this." Please ask yourself, though, where you would be if the Lord had any of these attitudes in His relationship with you. Are relationships important enough to you that you are willing to work through issues to be reconciled? It may take some hard, even grueling work, but I can guarantee you that it is worth it. Most often relationships are strengthened as individuals work through their tensions with one another.

Every so often individuals realize they had unrealistic expectations for the relationship and even though they work through the issues, which caused the tension, the friendship is not restored to what it had been. What I have in mind here is a dating relationship where tension occurs and the couple realizes that the relationship is not healthy. They may even follow biblical principles for reconciliation, but the relationship isn't restored. In fact they may end the romantic relationship but have a healthier, more realistic relationship as a brother and sister in Christ.

At this point it is probably pretty discouraging to be honest with yourself and admit you are struggling to practice some of the godly character traits explained above. In addition, perhaps you now see more clearly how some of the opposites of these character traits have been present in you and their presence has contributed to the tensions you now experience.

Let me remind you again that the gospel has embedded in it the power to change people and that your Savior came to heal the "broken-hearted" (Isaiah 61:1). Please submit yourself to doing things His way, even if it is painful to admit your part, and then you will see how the Lord can use this difficult circumstance that you find yourself in to accomplish his purposes (which most often are beyond our ability to comprehend (Romans 8:28; Ephesians 3:20-21).

Why Are These Character Traits Difficult to Practice

Earlier I posed the question of why we may struggle with some of these character traits. While there is truth to the existence of genetic disposition and how life's influences have shaped you to be who you are, we need to dig deeper into what Scripture teaches. Remember that if you have the attitude that others just need to accept you the way you are, you are not believing what Scripture says about growing into Christ-likeness (2 Corinthians 3:18). You are also stunting your potential for healthier relationships. To address why we struggle with showing these character traits we'll need to look at the bigger picture biblically. That will be the subject of the next chapter.

4

Jesus and the Heart of Conflict

While speaking to the religious leaders of his day our Lord made it very clear that the way we talk to others is directly related to the condition of our heart. Notice in the verses below the direct connection between the mouth and the heart. Also notice that another word for "heart" is "treasure." That will be significant later on in our study. Jesus said,

> You brood of vipers, how can you being evil, speak what is good? For the mouth speaks out of that which fills the heart. The good man out of his good treasure brings forth what is good; and the evil man out of his evil treasure brings forth what is evil
>
> (Matthew 12:34-35).

When looking at the character traits the topic of how we talk to others often came up. Words like "harshness" and "impatience" were used. But maybe your tendency when feeling tension in relationships is to *clam up*. Just as there are reasons why you speak impatiently, there are also reasons why you make the decision not to speak and perhaps even to withdraw from others during conflict.

Definition of the Heart

This topic is of utmost importance biblically and incredibly relevant to our discussion. The idea of the heart is discussed over a thousand times in Scripture. Understanding the nature of the heart, as it is revealed in Scripture, is as critical to our lives. Imagine a person who has a sore that will not heal even though ointments have been used repeatedly to try. While it's good to try to get the wound to heal wouldn't it be even better to find out why it's not healing? Maybe after some tests you would find out that this person has a cancer that needs to be treated not just at the skin level much deeper. So it is with us: until the deeper heart issues have been dealt with, there won't be healing and new sores will appear.

So what is the Heart, Biblically?

The Theological Wordbook of the Old Testament defines the heart as the

> *"richest biblical term for the totality of man's inner or immaterial nature....The three traditional personality functions of man; emotion, thought, or will."*[8]

"The heart" carries virtually the same meaning in the New Testament.

To summarize, the heart is your inner, immaterial person that is made up of your thought life, your emotions and your will. This means that your thought life reveals your heart. The decisions of your will reveal your heart. Your emotions tell you about your heart as well. This all becomes even more important if we take seriously Proverbs 4:23,

> *"Watch over your heart with all diligence, for from it flow the springs of life."*

It is clear, biblically, that the heart influences all we do and that includes how we handle conflict.

Hebrews 4:12 very clearly tells us that our

hearts have "thoughts and intentions." This verse illustrates the thought life and the will. If it is true that your heart is your mind, emotions, and will, you ought to see if you can prayerfully discern patterns in your thinking, decisions and your emotions during conflict to see what is truly going on in your heart. Another way of saying it is that your thought life tells you where your heart really is at during conflict. Your decisions reveal the true focus of your heart (for example, do you decide to avoid people you are upset with?) and your emotions are a vivid picture of what's happening on the inside (for example, are you afraid of what the person might say if you bring up your concerns?).

Since the heart is also about the thoughts, intentions, and will, it makes sense to say that there are things my heart wants. I think about the things I *want*. I make decisions related to the things I *want* and my emotions are especially strong when I don't get the things I *want*. Another word for wants would be *desires*.

It's All about Worship

Worship is an Old English word that originally was pronounced "worthship."[9] Therefore, it is accurate to say that that to which I ascribe worth is what I worship. Let's ask some questions that reveal what we ascribe worth or value to: What am I serving? What am I devoted to? What am I trying to get others to bow down to? What do I love? What do I talk about? What am I willing to sacrifice for?

We saw above that the word "treasure" is used in conjunction with the word "heart" in Matthew 12. My inner person is described as both my "heart" and my "treasure." How do you tell when someone treasures something? Wouldn't the list of questions be the same as the ones listed above?

Let's now tie together the idea of heart and worship. The Lord wants to be Lord over my mind, will, and emotions, and because of the gospel he is transforming my mind, will, and emotions to be like his. This lordship starts in my heart (mind, will, emotions) and the heart is the place where my treasures live. So what do your thinking, decision making, and emotions reveal about who or what is truly lord of your life. What are you treasuring?

Our lives are to be lived as one continuous act of worship; whether eating, drinking, we are to do all to the glory of God (1 Corinthians 10:31). The Lord is to be the One we primarily desire to serve, are devoted to, bow down to, show love toward, talk about and sacrifice for. He is to be our greatest treasure.

Changing the Focus of your Heart

Perhaps you now realize that your heart is in the wrong place. Yet there is hope! You can change! I often tell the students in my counseling classes, "If false worship is the problem, true worship is the solution." In other words, figure out what the opposite of the false worship is and start to practice that, and true worship will then replace the false worship. Sometimes this happens quickly, but most often it takes place over time.

Let's examine three common heart themes that feed conflict: living for the approval of people, desiring to be in control, and loving comfort.

Living to Please People: Treasuring the Opinions of Others over the Lord's

During times of conflict the person with this heart theme is afraid to speak, or will say things just to please people. This person can be consumed with thoughts of worry about what the other person is thinking. Thoughts like this fill this person's mind: "What will they think of me if I say what I really believe?" Rather than talking this person may clam up.

Desiring to be in Control: Wanting Others to Do What You Want Them to Do

The thought life of this person can be dominated by such things as "How do I get others to do what I would like them to do?" This person may even joke, "If others would just follow my ideas, the world would run more smoothly!" This person gets upset when his or her plan isn't followed or when others don't seem to respect his or her opinion as much as he or she thinks they should. Life can seem "out of control." This person's communication with others are taken as orders. The tone of voice can often be harsh.

Loving Comfort: Treasuring Relaxation and a Hassle-Free Life over the Reality That Life Includes Conflict

The person who struggles with this type of heart theme usually sees conflict as a major hassle because he or she just wants life to be fun and relaxing. This person might be thinking about the person he or she is in conflict with, "Why can't they just relax and not make such a big deal out of things?"

Each of these heart themes reveals false worship because something is being treasured above the Lord. They are not the responses of a person who is worshiping the one true and living God.

There are many things that could be said concerning how to combat each one of these in particular, but they all have a common theme: they have a low view of the Lord.[10] The people-pleaser is more concerned about what others think than what his or her Lord thinks. The control-freak can get obsessed with keeping life under control, while forgetting that there is a sovereign Lord over all the earth whom we are to trust. The comfort-lover has a small view of life. If the comfort-lover could get a bigger view of what his or her life is about before the Lord, he or she wouldn't be as consumed with taking it easy.

A generic way to combat all three of these false worship positions is to actually worship the greatness of who our Lord is. I really mean *worship*. Notice I didn't say, "Read about worship." I said *worship*. That means to meditate on, sing about, rejoice in, pray to, be thankful for, and read about how big our Lord really is. There are all kinds of tools the Lord has given us to do that, including Scripture, hymn books, theology books, and creation. But the key here is to *actually worship* the Lord, not just study about him. What will help your stubborn desires? It is replacing them through the power of the Holy Spirit with superior desires, and I believe that happens through worship. If false worship is the problem then true worship is the solution!

It is also very clearly an act of worship to do exactly what the Lord desires us to do. Back in Ephesians 4 he tells us what that is.

Actions That Result in Preserving the Unity of the Spirit

Paul writes in Ephesians 4:3 that all believers (not just the church leaders) are to

> [be] diligent to preserve the unity of the
> Spirit in the bond of peace.

Let's think about this in a little more detail. "Being diligent" means to "make every effort," and the expression is in the present tense in the original Greek, which implies that he is saying, "Continually make every effort to maintain the unity of the Spirit in the bond of peace." In other words, we ought to exhaust ourselves trying to keep peace and restore peace that has been broken by conflict.

We already saw that our Lord is highly relational and relationships are important to Him. They are so important that our heavenly Father sent his only Son to die in our place, paying the penalty for our sin so that we can be restored to relationship with our God! God is so concerned about us "making every effort" to restore broken relationships that He tells us in Matthew 5:23-24,

> "If therefore you are presenting your offering at the altar, and there remember that your brother has something against you, leave your gift at the altar, and go your way, first be reconciled to your brother, and then come and present your offering."

Relationships are so important to our Lord that he tells husbands that they need to

> "live with your wives in an understanding way... and show her honor... so that your prayers will not be hindered" (1 Peter 3:7).

I understand that to mean that if my relationship with my wife is not right, my relationship to my Lord is not correct either. Ouch!

How do you know if you have endeavoured to preserve the unity of the Spirit? Well, can you honestly say that you have exhausted all the biblical means you know for trying to be reconciled? At the end of this mini-book there is a list of resources that will give you many ideas for actions you could take to try to be reconciled.

A Reasons for Hope

Right now, you may feel hopeless. Maybe you've even tried to follow some biblical principles for resolving the conflict. It could be that you and your spouse have talked about the same issues over and over again, but don't seem to ever come to resolution. Let me give you some reasons for hope.

» Because we are in Christ and he is in us (Ephesians 1-3) we can conclude that we have new abilities to work through issues compared with those we had in our pre-salvation days.

» Because the Lord is in us we are capable of supernatural acts of forgiveness.

Conflict Provides Opportunities[11]

We can also feel hopeful because during conflict there are opportunities to address issues that wouldn't normally get addressed. We also have the opportunity to serve others in ways that aren't part of regular life and that follow the example of our Lord's washing feet (John 13:1-15)

My view of conflict changed when I started realizing all of the opportunities that tensions in relationships provide for addressing issues in my own heart and in ministry to others. Before accepting this principle my default response was to avoid conflict at all costs. Then I accepted that conflict is inevitable and comes into my life through the sovereign hand of God. Therefore, it needs to be managed for his glory. This was revolutionary for my leadership.

Heat Reveals Dross

Finally, we can feel hopeful because the Lord is up to something really big in our lives during times of intense pressure. The heat of conflict reveals impurities that wouldn't surface unless we were put under this type of pressure. God's ultimate purpose is to help us become more like his Son, our Savior! He uses the pressure to reveal to us areas where we are not like our Lord and teaches us how to be more dependent on him. I've often told others that seminary taught me how to understand Scripture, but conflict taught me how to walk with the Lord.

I hope you too can cling to the truth that the Lord is truly up to something good in your life as you go through conflict

CONCLUSION

I grew up as a "PK" (preacher's kid) and unfortunately during my teen years fulfilled the stereotype. I was a rebel! My heart was filled with extreme bitterness toward my father. He always seemed to have time for others, but I hardly seemed to be on his radar screen. Just one example will let you know just how bad it got. To get the full impact you need to understand a little about my father.

He was a World War II veteran, having fought under General George Patton as a .50 caliber machine gunner on the famous Sherman Tank. Fighting against the Nazis he saw much horror, but the worst came near the end of the war when his unit was involved with the release of a concentration camp. You have probably seen pictures of the emaciated prisoners. My father saw them in person. It is hard for me to imagine how my father must have felt when I would say "Sieg Heil" and give him the Hitler salute when he would ask me to do just about anything.

But our gracious Lord had other plans for my

bitter soul.

In the spring of my junior year of high school the Lord brought me to true saving faith. When I was five years old, I had prayed to Jesus to be my Savior, but in high school I realized I was not truly saved. There was no evidence of heart change. Thankfully, at age seventeen, while attending meetings at a local church, the speaker gave an altar call to receive Christ. Even though I was under intense conviction of my sin, I did not respond. Instead I walked to my sister's home about half a mile away and told my sister that "I don't think I'm really saved." She very wisely did not try to "give me the assurance of my salvation" by reminding me of the prayer I prayed at the age of five. Instead, she explained to me the Good News of Jesus Christ as if it was the first time I had heard it. This time I fully recognized my sin. I knew that I was in the process of ruining my life and only God could save me by his grace. That night I confessed my sin, and he forgave my sin based upon his death and resurrection (Acts 26:20; I Cor. 15:1-3).

Almost immediately I felt convicted of my rebellion, and it was not very long afterwards that I went to my father and asked his forgiveness. However, I still had not dealt with the bitterness in my heart. About a year later, I went away to

Bible college and while there took my first biblical counseling class. In that class the professor was teaching through Ephesians 4, which we have been studying in this mini-book.

We had already studied what Paul said about putting off the old man, being renewed in the spirit of the mind, and putting on the new man (4:19-24). The following verses are just an extension of this principle. Paul writes,

> "Let all bitterness and wrath and anger
> and clamor and slander be put away from
> you, along with all malice. Be kind to
> one another, tender-hearted, forgiving
> each other, just as God in Christ also has
> forgiven you.

I sure was ready to get rid of my bitterness since it was eating away at my soul, but I remember thinking, with a little frustration, "How do you just stop being bitter." I realized then that this was not what Paul was saying. He was telling us to put off the bitterness by making a decision to forgive based upon the forgiveness we have received in Christ and then to replace it with acts of kindness and love. It is a whole package. To the Romans, Paul had written,

"Do not be overcome by evil, but overcome evil with good."

(Romans 12:21)

The put ons (verse 32) kill the put offs (verse 31) when done with the right motive.

The correct motive is extremely important and is directly related to Paul's phrase, "be renewed in the spirit of your mind" (v.23). Paul is essentially saying, "Be renewed in the inner person of your heart," since "heart" and "mind" are both inner-person words. He is telling us that the "thoughts and intentions" of our hearts can and should change because of who we are in Christ. Since we have been forgiven we can choose to "send away"[12] other's offenses.[13] So I went to work putting the whole process into practice, and within two months the bitterness of my soul was gone!

I am happy to say that through diligent work over the remaining years of my father's life we were able to have a loving relationship. My father is now with the Lord, but one of the last Sundays I was with him I sat on the side of his bed as he was suffering tremendously and read Scripture to him. We sang hymns together and listened to a message preached by Dr. John MacArthur. What a radical change from when I was a teenager! This is because of the power of the gospel and the obedient practice of biblical principles.

So please don't allow relationships to wither. Just as God in Christ has pursued you and forgiven you, please do so with others. You can get a good start by doing the Personal Application Projects at the end of this book.

My Closing prayer

Father of grace, I cry out to you for wisdom to know how to deal with tension and brokenness in relationships. I know that you are the expert on dealing with relationships, and I thank you for giving us an abundance of guidance in your Word. I pray that my brothers and sisters would now by your grace and in the power of the Holy Spirit discipline themselves to do what your Word says as an act of worship to you. This I pray in the name of our Savior, the Lord Jesus Christ, the Prince of Peace, Amen.

Personal Application Projects

Prayerfully meditate on the list of character traits and their opposites given in Chapter 3, and ask yourself which two you need to work on the most. How will you do it?

Then reflect on the following questions related to your heart:

QUESTIONS CONCERNING YOUR MIND

▶ What thoughts go through your mind regularly related to the person you are in conflict with or the situation in general? What do these tell you about your desires?

QUESTIONS CONCERNING YOUR WILL

▶ What decisions have you made regarding the conflict?

▶ What situations do you tend to avoid?

QUESTIONS CONCERNING YOUR EMOTIONS

▶ What do you fear in relation to the conflict?

▶ What makes you angry as you think about the conflict?

▶ List the things that worry you about this situation? What does this tell you about where your inner person is?

QUESTIONS CONCERNING YOUR INNER DESIRES

▶ What do you want that you're not getting?

▶ What are you getting that you're not wanting?

▶ Based upon how you've answered your questions, what patterns are you seeing in your heart? What word phrases would describe the heart theme that reveals what you are treasuring? (For example, "desires for control," "desires to protect self," "desires to keep people happy," or "desires for a carefree life.")

▶ What are the top two things you need to do based upon what you have read? When will you do them?

▶ Write a prayer of confession and commitment to the Lord based upon what you have learned.

▶ What are your expectations telling you about your perceived rights?

▶ Using Psalms 42-43 as a model, write your own prayer of lament to the Lord concerning the tensions you are feeling in relation to others.

▶ Matthew 7:1-5 the Lord admonishes us to get the "log out of our own eye first." After answering some of the questions above, list ten ways you have contributed to the conflict. If you're having a hard time seeing your part of the conflict, I recommend you read Chapter 2 of Ken Sandes's *Peacemaking for Families* (see "Where Can I Get More Help?" section) and answer the questions at the end of that chapter.

▶ What questions do you need to ask of the person you are in conflict with that would get at his or her "interests?" What is this person concerned about? What are his or her fears?

Where Can I Get More Help?

BOOKS

Baker, Ernie, *Men Counseling Men*; Chapter 16, "Helping Men Resolve Conflict" (Eugene, OR: Harvest House, 2013)

Jones, Robert, *Pursuing Peace* (Wheaton, IL: Crossway, 2012)

—*Uprooting Anger* (Phillipsburg, NJ: 2005)

MacArthur, John, *The Freedom and Power of Forgiveness* (Wheaton, IL: Crossway, 1998)

Poirer, Alfred, *The Peacemaking Pastor* (Grand Rapids, MI: Baker, 2006)

Sande, Ken, *The Peacemaker: A Biblical Guide to Resolving Personal Conflict* (Grand Rapids, MI: Baker, 2006)

—*The Leadership Opportunity: Living Out the Gospel Where Leadership and Conflict Intersect* (Billings, MT: Peacemaker Ministries, 2009

—*Peacemaking for Families: Managing Conflict in Your Home* (Carol Stream: IL: Tyndale House, 2002)

Strauch, Alexander, *If You Bite and Devour One Another* (Littleton, CO: Lewis and Roth, 2011)

Tripp, Paul David, *Dangerous Calling* (Wheaton, IL: 2012)

WEBSITES

Association of Certified Biblical Counselors (www.biblicalcounseling.com)

Christian Counseling & Educational Foundation (www.ccef.org)

Peacemaker Ministries (www.peacemaker.net)

END NOTES

1 "Strike the shepherd—Losing Pastors in the Church" by Ken Sande, found at the website of Peacemaker Ministries: http://www.peacemaker.net/.

2 Not Peacemaker Ministries. I became interested in Peacemaker Ministries because of this situation.

3 I am indebted to Ken Sande for this type of thinking.

4 Francis Foulkes, *Ephesians, The Tyndale New Testament Commentaries*; Grand Rapids: Wm. B. Eerdmans, 1989, 116.

5 Ken Sande, *The Peacemaker* (Grand Rapids: Baker Book House, 2006), page 204

6 Wayne Grudem defines progressive sanctification as a "progressive work of god and man that makes us more and more free from sin and like Christ in our actual lives." Systematic Theology (Grand Rapids: Zondervan, 1994), 746.

7 All definitions are from A Greek-English Lexicon of the New Testament by William Arndt, F. Wilbur Gingrich, Grand Rapids: Zondervan 1963.

8 Andrew Bowling, *Theological Wordbook of the Old Testament, Vol.* I; "Lev" (Chicago, Ill: Moody, 1980), 466.

9 www.thefreedictionary.com, "weorthscipe" Old English for "worthship." Accessed March 15, 2013.

10 Lord (capitalized) is being used here as in the Old Testament sense of the one true and living God as contrasted with idols.

11 Please read *The Peacemaker* by Ken Sande for a full discussion on this topic.

12 One of the Greek words for forgiveness is aphemi which means, "to send away." It is a decision we make.

Books in the Help! series include...